For Mike —
Best wishes & congratulations
on all your good work for
the Queens MFA —
Ji

WE ARE THE BUS

D1478928

JAMES McKEAN

James

Texas Review Press
Huntsville, Texas

FIRST EDITION, 2012
Requests for permission to reproduce material from this work should be
sent to:

Permissions
Texas Review Press
English Department
Sam Houston State University
Huntsville, TX 77341-2146

Acknowledgements:

Grateful thanks to the following journals in which poems first
appeared:

Agni	*Natural Bridge*
Artful Dodge	*Poet Lore*
Clackamas Literary Review	*Poetry Daily*
Cold Mountain Review	*Poetry East*
Crab Creek Review	*Poetry Northwest*
Crab Orchard Review	*River City*
Crazyhorse	*Southern Poetry Review*
The Georgia Review	*The Southern Review*
The Gettysburg Review	*The Texas Observer*
The Iowa Review	*The Texas Review*
Memoir	*Voices on the Landscape*
Motion: American Sports Poems	

Special thanks to William Ford, Robert Grunst, Alan Michael Parker, and
Paul Zimmer for their friendship and for their reading my work with care
and critical insight. And my gratitude and affection for our Iowa City
writing group, Julie Hanson, Jan Weissmiller, Kathy Hall and Dan Lechay.
Thank you. I still look forward to meeting after all these years.

Cover image: "Waiting 48" by Brett Amory
Cover design by Sara T. Sauers
Author photo courtesy of Meryl McKean

Library of Congress Cataloging-in-Publication Data

McKean, James.
   We Are The Bus / James McKean. -- 1st ed.
      p. cm.
   ISBN 978-1-933896-84-7 (pbk. : alk. paper)
   I. Title.
   PS3554.R437V54 2011
   811'.6--dc22
                                    2011005589

for Penny

CONTENTS

I.

II.

III.

I

LUCKY LOUIE

1/4/98

The old men in my family are gone,
the last, my uncle, ashes now
slipped by his wife and daughters
into the Sandy River.
He told me once stand here, fish there.
Now it is a winter without ice yet
but years since he and I cast to shadows.
When I saw him last,
he stood at the window, hands on the sill,
as if the frost-lined glass held
steelhead returning — sea-run and shining.
I did no more than nod
when he said try this and fish these —
a tangle of hooks and flashers,
plugs still in their boxes,
a whole vocabulary of bells and spoons,
his most tempting lures barbed,
a paper sack full of what might be,
of what he could imagine.
And when I showed my mother
what he had given me,
she lifted from my sack a #5 Lucky Louie.
Something behind her flashed.
She turned the wooden plug,
its treble hooks, its two eyes
iridescent, and said how angry
she had been at my father's wasting
pay on leaders and entry fees
and a Lucky Louie just like this one.
"He left me that morning
in our no-bedroom apartment," she said,
then showed me the Times clipping

where my father grins, his head
covered with hair, a 24-pound king
in one hand and in the other,
the keys to their new red DeSoto,
second prize in the Elliott Bay Salmon Derby.
My mother smiles beside him.
It is 1941. They are beautiful before the war.
They have a car, no children yet.
The box I hold says "Minser Tackle Company,
Aurora Avenue, Seattle 33, Washington"
and "Lucky Louie All Yellow, Price $1.75."
As of five days ago I am the oldest man
in my family. The treble hooks
are sharp after 57 years,
and the printed instructions, mine now,
replete with guarantees.

GIFT

It's the Tibetan prayer wheel I asked for—
bone handle beneath a tin cup,
embossed lid, the spinning weight
a chip of rebar on a ten-link chain.
Inside I find a paper scroll,
maybe The Dharma but what Sanskrit
do I read? So I roll it back around
the axle, around which all is supposed to turn.
But waving my hand back and forth
doesn't work and shaking pops
the lid off, the weight flopping like the stone
I threw long ago at our neighbor's house,
too young to know how off
my aim was, that old woman, I remember,
calling my father.
                    Oh, I prayed then
for the sun to rise once more, the moon to go full,
the sky to wheel around Polaris,
the only star that stood still above my turning
arms out on a warm summer night.
I wanted fall next then winter then spring launching
wind devils and new buds into leaves.
I found out it didn't matter what I wanted.
The moment at hand was my father's hand
turning me front and center.
But come on, what's new about falling down,
a ruler whacking your palm, a teacher
not your mother? Every time your face is slapped
it's the first time. Keep waving.
When the weight spins, life goes well well well,
and your axle squeaks.

MR. MOON

We aimed toward the light
in his garage, riding bikes
hard for the wind,
then coasting free
to skid, pivot foot down,
around his circular drive, Mr. Moon
on his porch, drinking coffee,
his dog silent. No wife.
Who is he? our parents asked
over barbecues. The man
who grinds glass, we said,
who wears his sleeves
rolled, who doesn't smoke.

Warned to stay away,
we watched from the road,
his drive, his window, the door
to his garage, the light
above a 50-gallon drum he circled,
two hands on a disc as red
as a mother's rouge.
He scooped carborundum
from small tins,
then emery and oxides,
and set a glass disc on a glass disc.
With his hands he copied
the shape of a rose to grind and polish.
We are pendulums, he said,
a red bandana tied around his head.
The world turns around us.

Silvered, his mirrors bent light.
He tested his work with knives

and shadows. One day,
he said, he would take us
through his eyepiece into the sky,
and when we looked back,
we would know at last
the names of stars and how
the new moon is dark and invisible
and pulls our parents from their houses
like the tide.

CLINKER BOAT

Much later, I knew "clinker"
meant cedar planks hand sawn,
brass nails driven through, bent over,
and seams lapped so tight
he caulked them with water.
On oak seats three miles
off Everett, the Sound rolling by,
we fished all day,
my hands deaf with cold,
the dime he placed on the seat
before me mine the second
I landed something worthwhile.
I doubted the cut-plug herring,
pleading now please
to the ignorant waves, possessed
by what ten cents could buy.
I was sure "clinker" meant
one mistake after another
like his jammed reel,
nylon blooming in his hands,
his swearing as mistimed
as the fouled Evinrude
that drove us here.
I never caught a thing.
But if I'm lucky now, I'll find
a dime on fire
in the corner of a room
where he sleeps in a chair he made,
his pipe lolling, embers
spilling onto the rug.
I'll tamp that fire out, remembering
how he hooked something deep
and worked it hand over hand,

its sides flashing silver.
Then I'll net it sure and bright
as a thought worth saving,
a dime to keep in my pocket
for all its lovely burning.

QUICKSILVER

The brass showed through...
      —Huck Finn

If I hadn't dropped
the Walking Liberty fifty-cent piece
on my way home, I never
would have discovered
the art of making a buck.

I was twelve. The old man
up the street elected me
to mow his new lawn
on a Saturday morning
warm enough for baseball.

All enterprise I raked
and bagged clippings for hours,
then reported in to receive
my shiny fifty cents,
so heavy in my pocket

I had to see it just once
before the ritual deposit
Monday morning with Mrs. Sullivan
at North City Savings and Loan.
Oh, I remember the thud

when my new cash hit the road.
Dented. A dud. All lead
when I bit into the hem of Miss Liberty.
How could this be? I trusted in God
and mysterious words.

If I spent it right now, I thought,

who'd know? The grocer,
Mr. Ruland? Mrs. Sullivan,
who called me sir?
Well, I'd know. That's who.

Thus, my first lesson in making a buck:
The truth isn't worth ten U-Nos.
The second: Art stays with you
because you can't spend it,
hiding it instead in your top drawer

for misery, for being the fool.
Years later, brow scrunched,
I stumble on the phony
and turn it over and over, wondering,
who made it, it's that good.

Maybe his mintmark—
the little "g" under "TRUST"—
stands for "garage" where he hid
his bullion and sand cast
each bogus four bits.

No bona fide half-dollar
could conjure such a story,
our artist obsessed
with getting his reeds right,
the blanks trimmed and sized

before he hand-coated each draft
with mercury, the Roman god
of commerce and thieves.
Quicksilver, our artist would say,
that incredible shine

so taking a boy long ago

in the light of a Saturday morning,
that new money slipped from his fingers
and he got the message
when Miss Liberty walked away.

'56 BUICK

When better automobiles are built,
Buick will build them.

It was my first—thirty bucks down
and thirty later—a land yacht, portholes
port and starboard. Not mere transportation, no,
but ride-engineered on a four-coiled,
deep-oiled, torque-tubed keel.
I had two keys. I had variable pitch dynaflow
beneath acres of seats, rolled and pleated,
the wheel Bakelite, the windshield panoramic,
the world tinted for my getaway.
Come on. Everyone's plum of an automobile,
it took hours to start. Whistles. Eyebrows raised,
I imagined, before *Buick* big, my Doppler

drop, eminence, merit in two tones,
might marshalled with consummate ease. Come on.
In deep and roomy comfort, I'd be on my way,
road master, all fenders and high beams.
Oh, please, best of Buicks, most luxurious of Buicks,
I was ready to plow, seventeen, running on talk:
Come on. Come on. Come on—
hiccup and roar. Look out.
Four sawdust tires, a gallon of gas, and I was linguistic,
out of reverse and in drive behind
three-hundred twenty-two cubic inches of high-
compression, every spark advanced.

RACKET BOX

Elvis on the radio,
our station wagon yawed like a tanker
toward Mukilteo where a clinker boat
would motor us to Hat Island,
the red, white, and blue Racket Box
in my lap, my father's voice flaring
with second thoughts ever since he laid out
$6.95 at the Kiwanis' fireworks stand
so I might be heard for once
as well as seen. He gave me the weekend
to light it all—Black Cats,
two-inch Zebras, the intricate braid of fuses,
mortars, Lady Fingers and the buzz
bomb's razzle bang.

For three days
I built and destroyed. No chrysanthemums,
water falls or girandoles for me,
who'd written to Cape Canaveral
for pictures, who'd cut match heads off
all winter and burned them in a dish,
who'd mixed saltpeter, charcoal
and sulfur in the attic to ignite the days,
anything to rocket past orders
and curfews before the inevitable and sad re-entry
into my own life.

I had three days
for serious demolition, every outhouse stirred,
tin cans bulged, revolutions ended
or begun by Big Chiefs or Yankee Boys,
even uncles launched when the wind blew
the final, show-stopping mortar over,

its eighth-pound TNT charge
skipping up the boardwalk underneath their porch.

That weekend
I held the punk, reduced every tyranny
I suffered to shredded paper, my hair
blown back, the smell of powder silver
and acrid on my hands, only a fingernail lost
despite what I was told. And despite what I was told
I smuggled three cherry bombs home
simply to hoard, independence won
on Independence Day, but couldn't resist
one late-night, back-yard, dog-barking explosion
or telling my mother the next evening,
no, it wasn't me, and don't be cruel and alright mama,
I'd mosey to bed when the King was done on TV.
How I wish I'd remembered to light that fuse
        and get away
from my father's palm, the report
still ringing in my ear.

TRANSFER

Fifteen means a new school
and remedial art class, the only vacant seat
behind the utility island, its paper
towels and sinks next to Lloyd Swain
who looks thirty, sleeves rolled
over muscles and blond hair DA'ed,
who hasn't said a word
since I arrived because Buddy Wilkins started
talking at me the moment
I sat down. I'm from Seattle. He doesn't care.
He's gonna kick my ass,
he says if I breathe. Now what?
                                    Mr. Boettcher,
the art teacher football coach, is leaving us
for ten minutes on our best behavior,
the opening Buddy looks for, a skinny
and pimpled version of Lloyd Swain,
in thick glasses and Vitalis hair.
Standing over me, his fist balled,
Buddy says push that milk ticket he dropped
at my feet with my nose all the way
to the door or he'll knock
my teeth out. I can't
move, folded up in my folding chair.
When I whisper "no," Buddy rears
and Lloyd looks up from years of water colors
and coil pots and says "Sit down,"
in a voice basso before I was even born
and "Pick up that ticket."
Buddy coughs, "Ok, Lloyd. Sure thing, Lloyd.
Anything you say, Lloyd,"
his Levis suddenly too big, cuffs rolled up
over his shins.

Let me say,
it wasn't courage. My legs wouldn't work.
"You got a locker?" the only thing
Lloyd will ask me the next two years.
Isn't there always fear? In the hallway?
In the parking lot? Behind the Frisco Freeze
where names are made—Chic Frissel,
Jim Allotta, Loren Porsch, Dean Lloyd,
Squire Tomassi whose glass-pack mufflers
announced him two blocks before
first period and its spit wads, the hallways
turbulent and suspicious all the way
to Mr. Boetcher's art class where I found
a needle to make my name,
bloody pins holes on the back of my wrist
where the skin was thick.
I'm the Marlboro man, I imagined,
and rubbed in India ink,
an art project I couldn't turn in
and hid beneath my watch for forty years,
the "J" finished, the "M"
off-center, half-done forever, because
when you're fifteen, the bell always rings.

FIVE STORIES

My Golgotha out the bus window,
the diving board at Morton Lake rose five stories
on four telephone poles, monument
to legends floating the high school hallways—
intestine flattening belly flops, swan dives
into the dock, and all those red-headed big-word
braggadocios who never surfaced again

even in memory. The man with chest scars is who
I remember, thinking as I peered up, wooden
ladders crisscrossed and cirrus bound,
that such heights would fall to courage and will.
Then here he came, up-side down, buzz-cut first, tattoos
a blur, arms clamped to his sides and only his words
right side up, "You owe me," he said eyes open two feet

above the water he parted like a plow, his girlfriend
watching at the edge of the dock because he'd said
stand here and listen and she did and his tidal wave
washed her lit cigarette clear to the parking lot.
I can do this I thought and climbed, eyes fixed on
one step at a time, the lake going small,
but I didn't figure on the wind or my wobbly knees

or the line behind me or birds circling
my feet as I reached the railing's end, the board
swaying. I could see for miles, the smoke of Tacoma,
the glint of the bay—and I shouldn't have
looked down. Air gone, my stomach gnawing, I swear
the lake was Kristine Alskog, my mouth open
in her presence, the sun brilliant off her whitecaps.

Here she was again in her dad's new Thunderbird

and I on the sidewalk's edge and here she was rolling
the window down, leaning across the seat
     in her dancing tights,
asking if I'd like a ride, and here she was smiling,
her breasts lifting as she leaned for the lock. Sweet Jesus,
I couldn't breathe all the way down, feet first,
ankles crossed this time for my cold inevitable reentry.

DANCE CONTEST

Me? who looked the other way,
sipping beer at the back
of Steemy's Bar and Grill on Thursday—
the dance contest night I failed
to notice on the marquee. She worked
her way toward me, the beautiful dancer
I'd admired from a distance
in her brief costume beneath the air-brushed
blue light and strobe. Such
blemishlessness I stared at I admit
but why fish me out of the crowd
by the hand for that night's
contest, her new partner, her foil, her less
than equal, left foot after
left foot, a bumbler on weak knees,
the disillusioned half of couple
number three now on stage beside the band
and two-piece jungle gym
where she sat sweating on my lap,
waiting our turn? Unless to tell me
more than I wanted to know
in the dim half-light, to let me dance
whatever I wanted, to let a fool grow
wise in drum rolls and cymbals and hard bass.
I was the fool and for her I jumped
and twirled, legs kicked out
in a latter-day galliard, and for her mended
stockings and wig, her bruised knees
and loose-thread rhinestones, the rings
on her fingers, her husband's truck on I-80,
her two kids home with a sitter,
for her dancer's shoes worn at the heel,
for the sweat of her brow, I fell

to one hand, ran around it double time, circling
once, flipped, kicked, the splits
a mistake but recovered, twirled her in hand, a mix
of cakewalk, half-polka & cha-cha,
a newly invented half-baked
Thursday night fever, a layman's leaping
beyond the self for Nancy,
her name that night, for the spotlight and cheers,
for the ten bucks we won split two ways
and a pitcher of beer. She picked me
and I went to my knees for her,
for rain, for the harvest—three minutes' worth
remembered as love.

GOOD NEWS BLUES

I'm not myself whoever that is 7 o'clock Saturday morning.
   but here I come—the doorbell
redemption's alarm—stumbling foot over foot down
   the stairs to rip the door, eight-gauge chain
and dead bolt first, out of its jamb, me, a ham-fisted,
   sleep-starved Polyphemus,
who finds nobody in the blinking light but this girl—
   mother pushing at her shoulder—holding up
her last inky copy of what's in store.
   Oh, it's the *Good News* blues.
A lamb of lambs before me and my stomach growls, so
   forgive me like your paper says,
my blurry eye and holey shirt inside out.
   I've suffered an evening in this world
and a night of dreaming and offer only my dog hair
   this morning and no shoes, a musty house, the door
hung awkward. I'm yours, mouth breathing and
   bone grubbing,
   my dust rising in the light of your brilliant appeal.
Please. There's no face bold enough to help me focus.
   Give me
   a minute before eternity, something in single syllables
like "thick" and "fog." It's early beyond comprehension
   and later than I think. I know, I know.
My pants are misbuttoned and my breath is sour.
   I like a good abstraction as well as the next
somnambulist, ears ringing, sunlight like a cymbal
   on the wall, but help me here—a shower and coffee
might save me from myself, then a word or two to savor
   before ecstasy. How's the family?
How's the garden growing? Thanks for dropping by.

A "T" IN THE ROAD

There's singing in the wind.
From her cell phone the neighbor's new wife calls
to say her horse is loose, headed toward you,
and would you help? Outside
you stand in slippers like a son-in-law—
everything you own owed to the future—and survey
your little leg of fenced road,
totem that you are, amateur watchman
of this place, rooted until a horse whinnies, shuddering.
Now the widow who lives around the corner
and tends geese, rises from her garden,
shears in one hand, straw hat
tied beneath her chin, this woman in half glasses—
someone's aunt who understands
the thousand mysteries of grammar—
waves her apron until the horse turns
to find Mr. Ruland, the retired locksmith,
who collects coins and pulled engines,
who holds himself up with his cane,
who waits everyday for the mail.
Even he three-legs his way
outside and there they stand, serifs
on the cross of the "T." Now the horse turns
down your road, descending, unfettered.
Wouldn't this horse rather run
the plains, sweat and climb the hills that fade
into the simple browns of afternoon?
Think of places named for directions,
        one leading to the next.
Think of what's been asked, of what
you've promised. There she is, your neighbor's wife,
out of her car, running,
rope halter in hand. You hear cardinals
and step into the road.

II

FAMILY REUNION, 1959

How could this grown man,
a stranger, love my aunt's blushing?
In a herd of cousins
I chafed in loafers, a white shirt,
absurdity my first
starched collar. Here, relatives
in name only, this roomful of near kisses,
a wasted afternoon. Grandmothers
sat behind their fat arms.
My mother played the organ.
He sang, "Home Again," hung
on my father's shoulder—drink spilling,
shirt untucked, a dog howling—
and wept. I couldn't stay.
I couldn't leave and begged
the day shorter, the hallway so full
of strangers he might never
find me to kiss me and praise
nothing I had done
and weep for a life I had
yet to live. "No relation of mine,"
I boasted in the car going home,
and spoke ill of him
until my father mentioned
Iwo Jima and "enough."
It meant nothing.
But since then I've learned
to read beyond myself and imagine,
why our family fed him—
my stupidity and fear ignored—
and why they held him and were kissed by him,
one of our own.

NIGHT TERROR

Before any words, the crying out
as if something infinite
measures her hands' orbit,
as if the molecules of air she breathes
grow huge. No wonder
she cries, no words
for this but "oh" before the shriek.
It is all we can do to wash
her hands with towels,
to walk her back to the room
she dresses in each morning
then down the stairs,
the lights on so she might wake
and find herself back
in the small world we give her,
so she takes words
and cold water for her tongue.

ANONYMOUS CALLER

The line is open for her.
We lay the receiver down
so she might hear what little
transpires now that hello is
understood and *who is it?*
a question we no longer ask.
She has never said a word.
Our fridge kicks in. The patio
door rumbles open, sheet rain
crackling against the window,
a sound like fire maybe
over the thin line that leads
to her room where she listens,
we imagine, knees up, hugging
pillows. Three days, maybe four
later on her rag rug, next
to Kleenex, her make-up kit,
a card to weep over—
she unties her big new shoes,
wondering where her body went,
and dials, for she has taken
her mother's phone, shut the door,
and turned the lamp down to shrink
her room until the dark holds her
small again. We hear bubbling
from her aquarium, its guppies
never named because that
would end them. We hear the bed
creak beneath posters of what
she fears she will never be—
happy, arms out, dancing
in a meadow full of friends
and harmless boys, their pants rolled,

her hat silly. We don't know
when she might call (though we know
she is twelve because we have
traced her) or why she chose our
number. No matter. She keeps
us on hold as if to keep
her new self at a distance.
We offer water running
in a sink, vegetables
snapped and cleaned, sometimes talk
of the morning or simply
our thoughts out loud when we ask,
How are you? to a silence
one day she too will outgrow.

RESCUE

Beside the pool a child
in diapers finds
her own reflection—mother
sleeping beneath a hat—
and falls without a splash.
The girl who watches
doesn't move, as if such falling
were simply rain
to step back from beneath
the jacaranda tree.
She holds her breath
for this child
until the father shouts
and mother wakes to pull her
from the water, crying.
Now in the girl
the child she was descends,
silent, the surface
left behind,
and now the woman
who she will be cries out,
the life she reaches for
aloud at last in rescue.

TIDE

The bay sits surface calm
above the undertow, the day warm,
the salt I taste swimming

familiar. Too far
from shore, adrift, I think
of my father long ago

sitting on the edge of his bed
in early afternoon—I was
young and this moment fit

nothing I understood
of weekdays in summer—
in his T-shirt,

a Kleenex held to his mouth,
and one drop of blood
falling onto the hardwood floor,

the sound a thump
like his fingertip on my head.
I am old enough

now to know his teeth
were pulled like his father's before him,
when "fix it" meant

all at once. I backed away.
He pulled his legs up
to lie down.

I've drifted far enough.

Fear like a tide makes me
crawl my way back. One day

I know I won't. It's true
and about time.

HORSESHOES

My father held thumb and forefinger
a quarter turn on the shank,
and two pounds of horseshoe
dipped and rose. Fond of city parks,

he preferred clay pits
but settled for backyard sand
stray cats peed in,
two hand-dug pits forty feet

stake to stake, out of sight
behind rhododendrons,
below the rock wall and ivy,
past the flower garden and lawn,

along the back fence near the compost
pile and stack of fence posts
where Mr. Nordheim, his competition,
who swore in Norwegian,

hid his aquavit. Always three-quarters
of a turn the shoe made
rising halfway and falling the rest,
a life of labor now easy

and exact. No need to grunt
or fling, they'd say. Make them
chickadees settling out of the air.
Follow through—back, arm, and fingers—

lightly in the last release.
Each knew how far and no farther
that stake was. Neighbors,
they took their turns,

shoe on top of shoe
until the last opened
the moment before the pit and
throughout my father's garden—

hydrangeas, the delicate asters,
the calla lilies he planted
for my mother—the wait and then
the ringing out.

GATHERING

Embarrassed she closes the door
and wipes her hands
on a dish towel and watches him
disappear through violets
blooming on her window shelf this warm
August morning—his sole-
flopping shoes, threadbare, paint-spattered,
sagging pants, the belt split,
shirt untucked and that salt-caked
baseball hat, his team long
defunct. He wanders alleys, his empty
coffee cans strung on wires,
this habitué of vacant lots, servant of the pluck
and gather, who forgives
the canes, who stoops, who sweats, unshaven
and gray, dusted and bleeding,
who sees beneath the undergrowth, who suffers
the thorns and hornets
and intractable pines, the sting and scuff,
the aching back and long
walk home at noon, a pilgrim kitchen bound
to leave his quarts and pints,
the morning stolen for himself, the blackberries
given to her, stain and blood
and old clothes shed at the door, her supplicant,
his thoughts on the possibility
of pie.

COME ALONG

Eighty years of wind
through branches, the weight
of mulberry leaves
until mortise and tenon
let go, until board and batten relax,
nails gone thin, rafters
and ridge board settled, walls
and their posts and beams spread,
the roof squatting, gravity's
insistence on the present and level.
How the burnishing rain
would bring this barn down
to one story, then none,
an architecture of the untold—
no more horses, no more hay,
the carriage on its thin wheels
and rigid axles dismantled.
But for ropes tied to beam heads,
south wall to north,
the come along's pull and pull
until yellow pine beams
travel one foot
for eighty years, the barn groaning
as if memory were an exercise
to suffer, a bad hip, a back
straightened, the roof raised inches
until walls go plumb enough
for new struts and collar ties.
Until the old lies braced,
the roof shingled to keep the rain out,
dust rising behind old glass,
reglazed though uneven since poured,
and the same light day after day
sweeps the floor.

A PLACE FOR EVERYTHING

When my mother spoke
of sadness and widows,
my father muttered "Well, well,"
and shook the paper open
in front of his face.

Now fifty years together
isn't enough. I was wrong about her,
a widow three days who will not
sit in his chair. I wait to lift
whatever she wants and then

as if I were a boy again wandering
at dusk I hear her voice fly
across the woods to call me home.
A place for everything,
I thought, was what she loved.

On their unmade bed—
a torn envelope, her birthday card
he must have hidden days ago
beneath his socks, signed in x's and o's,
a boy's hand, a boy's gesture.

Seventy tomorrow, she asks
for help tonight to sort suspenders,
trousers creased to their cuffs,
the two-tone shirts she chose for him
and washed and folded and set into a drawer.

SURROUNDED BY OWLS

The old men
I ate dinner with each Sunday,
my father-in-law,
his brother from Norway via North
Dakota, and a neighbor,
the oldest, his wife long dead—
centuries blinking—moved me slowly
by word, by nod, by their grasping
of arm rests and knees
collapsing so the last empty chair
rose straight-backed
in the middle of them, their glasses
wetted with scotch.
Sit, they said and I did
and listened mostly though once
I mentioned I woke
before dawn because an owl called.
Beneath the moon,
I cupped my hands to hoot back.
I heard snow collapse,
no wings, and a vertebra crack
in my spine—my notes rising up
until stars in oak branches
opened their great lids,
and the wind laid its cold talon
along my neck. "Yes," they said, "yes,"
and turned their heads toward me,
leaning as if to pray
because I had wandered so far
into the open.

GOOD "D"

—after Edward Hirsch

Their center blocks out and the ball
falls into his lap like the coach's book

says it will. Pivot, two-handed chest pass
to the outlet man, his flip

to the guard sprinting up the middle and the crowd
senses a break rolling at half court

and rises now for the finish, the jam
over a nondescript visitor

in knee wraps, invited to play in this gym
well lit on a Friday night in a state

that welcomes him and would send him home
bruised except he's hustled back

and turns in their key to wait—all taped fingers
and high tops—before the whole floor,

the forwards in their lanes pumping toward him
fast, two points on the stat sheets

written all over their faces, the guard dribbling
too high, head down as if he

needs a script, the guard who loves his right hand,
who pulls up late, who looks where he

passes, drunk on the home court's
din of expectation, everyone on their feet

for a goal good as given
over the nobody in his dull uniform

who stutter rushes the guard left, left
hand up, right down,

and releases the moment the pass is flung in panic,
the forward rising toward the basket

empty-handed because good defense reads well,
lives in the passing lane and lifts

the ball from beneath. Now, the forward,
who can't come down fast enough,

and the guard, suddenly tired, find far
up the floor the score turned,

the time gone and the crowd at a loss, fumbling
to sit back down, to say anything

for what's been stolen.

MY MOTHER-IN-LAW ARMS HERSELF

Her middle grandson, small caliber and
overcharged himself, thought something
more petite might give
comfort those long lonesome nights
so for a time his .32 automatic
lay loaded beside her late husband's
snub-nosed .38—two lumps
beneath her pillow and call anytime
he said and we'll practice and load the clips
and plink at tin cans.

Or shoot your neighbors, I argue,
but I'm on shaky ground here,
"reasonable" the least appreciated
of defenses and after all,
who's to say what she's aiming at?

The world she remembers these eighty
odd years has offered fine choices
in war outright or undeclared,
the neighbor's dog rabid, and great red clouds
to the east blistering each morning.

Why else dig those bunkers,
hoard those potato buds?
Her life, full of wishes
and foreclosures, lies like a neat hand
good girls practice in notebooks.
So one husband, four children,
thirteen dogs, a crowd of cats, hotels,
useless cars, soap operas and five houses
later mean that's enough.

Here's the line we fire from.
No more ambiguities,
no more faint praise,
no more coordinated outfits
and matching hats, no more
elaborate and fully sauced Sunday
dinners for the subordinates,
the relatives, the needy,
the ne'er-do-wells—for better or worse
the world shrunk to light-leaks
behind her silk sleeping mask.

"Who's there?" she asks, reaching
beneath her pillow,
the sun she can't see up for hours.

It's all too much and now
me again, having moved her guns
out of reach, unloaded and
locked up, another thing stolen from her
though she'll not mention that
and hates me for it.

POLICY

A friend of a neighbor visits
on a Saturday in spring
and my father sets two ones,
a five, then two dimes and two cents
on the table in the kitchen
of his new four-room house
on Dibble Street in Seattle, and signs
and dates the application
in black ink—I see 47 years later
his hand, white on the black
ammonia paper and mistake it
for my hand. Maybe he seals
the thought he could give no thought.
In three months I'll be two.
He has held his job one day,
a warehouseman it says, his house
needing order I remember him
saying, and here's help from Banker's Trust,
my life insured when death
is proved, the purpose X'd
by "clean up fund" and "savings."
What was he feeling, pen in hand,
a wife, a house, a new child, the war
over, the street he lives on oiled
finally and for once on an afternoon
he finds a blank space in his future,
the past given to a row of boxes
he checks—tuberculosis no, loss
of limbs no, insanity no, his child
healthy at three foot and 34 pounds,
their habits sensible at two drinks
a day, his appendectomy healed,
their lives as settled now as the seed

in their new lawn. He promises
we will not fly, that he will pay $7.22
four times a year so my life and its death
will lie bound by a serifed face and heavy paper,
engraved and watermarked
in a large building in Des Moines.
The promise of $1000 is typed.
There is a table of values, how
the years add up and what he must forfeit
if he were to change his mind,
which he doesn't, sitting back, the pen capped.
Half a century lies two years away
on the date of issue, April 1948,
after which I lived my life before him
indifferent, unaware he would
fear for me or fear that he had not
prepared, though insurance he admitted
later was a large word
best kept at the back of a drawer in the house
one day I would clean and order,
the policy on my death long expired,
though he left me his thinking and signature,
and they are benefit enough.

PANAMA HAT

When I tug the brim
and glance over my shoulder
at the mirror hung
on the hallway closet door,

I see my grandfather startled
and jowly, lips for once
without their Chesterfield brought near

to kiss me. I remember
his shiny hands, the skin transparent
when he placed them
on my shoulders and walked me

into the slow, domino-filled afternoon.
My mother would return
at five. I knew that

even though his new wife could bake,
my mother had banished them
to this tiny apartment.
and my two visits a year.

A grandfather, who paid
his rent in cash,
who waited down the hall,

shoes shined, a large
sleeve-gartered, solitary man
my mother told me to forget,
buried I don't know where but rising now,

a Panama hat hiding one eye,
the other in the mirror,
looking at me.

THE DUCK

You feed a spoonful of turkey
to your sister, younger but searching now
for every word. It's Thanksgiving

at the Greenwood Nursing Home.
She has forgotten me, her nephew,
but not you, Mother, always competent—

she the frivolous, pretty one you pointed out
in albums at home. Married, you fell
in step and worked. Not to be

outdone, she found her Russian,
a stranger who made tires and smoked too much,
hands hard as lug nuts, nails torn,

and that black-greased widow's peak pointing
wherever he stared as if his whole self
might vulcanize you. Even his gaze

in the black and white photo taped to the wall
beside the nurse's call button
reminds you of the hatchet

you found one Thanksgiving. How
he promised turkey and brought their duck instead,
white and flapping

in his creased hands, cigarette ashes
dropping onto your polished linoleum floor.
Oblivious, a pet—

you killed it in the backyard

and their kids cried through dinner.
They had to be fed, you explained—blood

on your apron and a spot
no one dared mention next to your eye.
Now you squint, your sister

more childish than ever, turning her head
away from the spoon. Come now. The men left
so long ago, you say, having tended

to yourself and now your sister.
There never has been enough food
to go around.

MOTEL

Don't swat the mosquitoes.
Call and we'll spray.
                    —The Management

We've traveled 600 miles,
Our U-Haul full of embarrassments
To find we don't listen
Even to each other. This room
Is anywhere, its water
Chrome, its air damp,
Its walls thin with the groans
Of those who sleep in separate angers—
Like us, quarreling
Over nothing, who find
No place to live, who cannot
Lie still for the whine
Circling our ears and must rise
Against the rules
And swat mosquitoes
Until they register our stay
On the white stucco wall.

ROOT BOUND

Your mother's plants suffer
a sag of forgetting.

Will you throw them out
or run a knife

between soil and clay?
Such blue violets

to last so long. Never mind
her knick-knacks,

her cups, her porcelain birds
perfect in flight—

not a doubt when you
gave these away.

But not so when you turn
each plant over

to shake it free—dirt
sifts through your fingers,

roots circling
tighter and tighter.

Who would have them
aside from you?

MIDDLESTAND FERRY

This far from shore
we are the largest measure
of ourselves, standing on deck or out
of the cold in the one cabin,
where a wall displays Lake Champlain
at its worst—no memory, it seems,
without loss and high winds.
Essex dwindles, its window lamps
a residue of horizon, the vague
Adirondacks above clapboard and tar shingles
smoking after rain. A bell sounds.
A plaque names this ferry the third
in a long line of crossings.
Our wake trails behind.
The wind in our faces.
It is April here. The sap runs
and snow turns to mud. The lake rises
to lift us all, the old saw says,
though we pay something
to stand here suspended
in our shoes, the diesel thrumming.
The bow cuts us toward low bluffs
riddled with birds,
and I worry how we will
line up, the wind shifting sideways.
I have a name, a map.
From here it's all I've got to go on,
the pilot drifting into the dock,
a road dropping down to lead us someplace
we'll discover soon enough.

III

CLIMBING ST PETER'S

All these steps I'm destined to descend,
    remembering the ascent as blessed, eyes on
the anointing rotunda light, lifting
    my knees foot by foot toward another heaven
on earth, my two minutes behind the holy brow—
    the dome of St Peter's, Giacomo della Porta's redo
of Michelangelo's circle on a circle, a shell
    in a dome and a long climb on a hot Roman day.
I promised myself puffing up I'd forget once and for all
    the neighbor's wife sunbathing in her back yard.
I'd eat less and wear sensible shoes and cut
    my stride, my feet newly modest and chaste
on granite steps, leaning as we climb, around and around
    as if parsing a Latin scholar's head. I promised
to do laundry twice a week, to allow my brother-in-law
    his new car, to leave coins in every bell
ringer's pot at Christmas. But if I thought myself forgiven
    after my allegory of short steps, fifty years
of transgressions overcome, sins left to a loss of breath,
    my knees weak with absolution, the city of Rome
before me and the future as simple as thin air,
    then I failed to see what lay ahead—the old man
luck gave me to follow single file back to earth,
    his wooden leg
    the stress in six hundred and fifty two iambs
down, a brick wall at each shoulder, past two windows,
    past the stolen obelisk, past the gallery of saints
bleeding copper, their hems all loose rivets. Down
    and around into the oven of everyday
we spiraled to a level in Dante, where traffic
    is ridiculous and pigeons dot the tables and waiters
in white aprons shout *mangia* to the newly saved
    and young women hold cigarettes above glasses
        of Campari
and turn their faces toward the sun.

WE ARE THE BUS

direct—Monteverde
to San Jose but stop if someone waves
or lifts a sack of onions bound
for relatives. My nephew
has taken your money.
Your seat is numbered by the window
you must open for the humid plain
and close on the dust. I am your driver.
I have rolled my sleeves
today and my brother rides along
standing clear to San Jose.
His boy took your suitcase.
The picture of our father, mercy
and blessings on him, rides the visor.
It is he who worked the fields
to buy this bus and we lay our hands
in blessing everyday on the wheel.
We have taped in red and white
every sharp corner every chrome rail
so our grip will be sound
all the way down the mountain's dirt
and shoulderless road. Please,
relax. This road is well-traveled.
It is the dry season. On each side of us
there are inches to spare beside
the cliff rising, the rainbow falling behind.
Trucks hear us coming and stop
for coffee, for we are the bus. We carry
everyone's sister home on Sunday.
You have your ticket. My brother tells me
when it is safe to pass on the left
or the right, to flick our lights
to sound the horn to say, please,

slow in reverence and pull aside
in prudence and raise a fist in greeting.
My brother admires how I shift
the plastic gear knob Virgin third
to fourth and find the open lane,
a shoulder and the ditch,
how we drop from cloud forests
through sugar cane and pineapple fields
into the city and its fireworks,
its crowded lanes, its blind corners
we turn on faith because
we are expected. We have 49 seats
and 75 souls and dry goods
and animals and spare tires.
We fill the town with exhaust.
We are the bus.

GEESE

It's hard to tell the purpose of a bird.
—Richard Wilbur

They are sand-bit and ornery,
protectors by habit and if
I thought them loyal, grateful for a job,
what's all this wail and squabble?
After work, home, reading the paper,
I'm set in my easy chair but
here they are, tapping at the front window, these
slug-eaters and browsers, lords
of their line of sight, shrill wives and malcontents,
web-footed usurpers ready
to nip at my cuffs, their note-scalding
hiss boiling over. No matter
if this place is horse-kicked and chicken-rifled,
all dirt road and back alley,
the horizon as tireless
as cars on blocks, the soil suspect,
the sprinklers muttering *tsk tsk tsk* to this two-
acre, tumbled, goat-pruned, sand-
blasted, weed-shot and willow-starved-beyond-weeping
paradise of pretending. They're all business,
honk "Get out here," mean to protect
me from myself, slippered,
newspaper in one hand,
feathered neck in the other so I might lift
six pounds of goose off the ground,
knowing what's good for it
is good for me, so I might explain bill to nose
that I live here, work's done,
let's have peace or I'll write
their remembrances with quills,
feast on goose, sleep under down,

to which they honk "That's better,"
raise their wings to the feather tips
and slap my cheeks until they flame.

TOOTH

I'm near the end as well so hooray
for this citizen who leaves his car in midtraffic
and climbs the hood of the car in front of him,
stopped in the lane next to me at a red light
in Oakland, California, on a hot summer afternoon.
He finally has his say, swearing through tomato-red
cheeks, fist balled and spitting. I keep
    my window rolled up
though I'd cheer if my mouth didn't bleed and words
didn't stumble from my numb lips. Today
I took a friend's advice but her well-meaning Italian-
born dentist, who believes in cleansing
by pain, could wrench my tooth out only at rush hour.
I made it on time but crawl back in traffic
that lines up like teeth. All I taste is iron and cotton.
I swear the radio plays opera from Milan,
a chorus of famous dentists come home, doing fifty
molars an hour, their gap-toothed relatives suffering
no more. I paid for his leverage. With his probe
he pointed out what I should let go and what I might keep.
I kept the memory of two breasts at eye-level
beneath the white, blood-spotted smock of Becky,
the assistant who winced on cue when my tooth cracked,
who caught it in a pan, who wrote my future
on a little card and wrapped my tooth in foil
like silver rigatoni, a relic, blessed with pliers,
and in her hands forever wise. Wait. I've found Daly City
to be a boundless stucco grin. Wait. The lady
in the car next to me doesn't move as if
the man jumping on her hood is full service,
doing a jig, conducting. I'd like to thank him.
I'm nearly home and will drink soup and lie down and
think of him, afoot at last in lane two, his wonderful

paroxysms of rage, who left his car behind
as if it were a bad tooth, the motor running and the keys
locked inside when the light turns green,
and we all drive off in a great crescendo of honking.

PILGRIMS

Your postmarks closer and closer
until you knock this windy day.
We have waited with towels,
syrups and salt. Our water is warm.
We hold your hands
that shaped our names and complained
in cursive beneath the crooked Chinese stamp.
Leave that pig misery behind,
we say, unwinding your blue scarf,
and speak to us of poppy fields
before the stone flower of Mount Kailash,
of walking and walking
until your bags lay here.
You spin in place, boots off.
Words. Now flesh. Ten thousand miles
for a tub, yours each year,
your hair longer, gray, braided,
wound twice. Water runs behind a door.
We imagine your unpinning, fingers
dressed with soap and permethrin,
our gift, until the holy lice of Lhasa
circle counter-clockwise
down the drain.

UWAJIMAYA

Beside sidewalk sweepers and seagulls in the early
   street, this morning's
first shoppers by ones and the still fortunate twos
   gather before the sun

rising in the market's windows. Seattle glistens,
   washed, its boats
pulling nets all night, the fish iced and boxed and
   trucked, the salmon,

blue fin, albacore, the boned, the predator and
   schooled, mollusks,
the shelled, cartilaginous and flat, whole or drawn
   in trays

behind the door open at nine by daughters and
   nieces and granddaughters.
Canes first, navigating beneath their hats, high-
   belted and sweatered,

these ancient shoppers with their wicker baskets
   gather before
their sons and nephews and grandsons who wait
   shoulder-to-shoulder,

aprons bloodied by early work, knives and steels
   belted, arms at rest
behind iced schools, Dungeness alive in the holding
   tank, butter clams,

oysters and blue-shelled crab, prices grease-penned
   for all but these venerable
shoppers who bow before the life-giving fish. What
   fine color, they agree,

how fresh the bright gills, orange roe, sequins and
    nacre, the red and the white flesh
cut clean behind those black unfocused eyes.
    Such bellies,

such useful fins, what aristocratic heads, what
    shame to waste
anything they say each morning. We will take them,
    they say, and they do,

the catch no others understand, made delicate by
    age and charcoal, by steam
fluted through bamboo, rice, vegetables—fish taken
    and given back—

and daughters and sons and their daughters and sons bow
    and praise them and bow again.

CAMP

Skogfjorden

On the back road, happy,
we bring you home from the north,
and hear you in the back seat sing
in Norwegian, explaining how
you stood with others before chairs and soup,
good bread and open faces and sang
for your hunger as you sing
now for us, vowels full of the sea and tides,
a gull echoing off a fjord's
granite walls rising steep into the light
that lasts all night all summer.
But it is late and dark here
and we live far inland before a simple horizon,
and as much as we missed you the long
drive south and east has left you
sleepy or is it the sheer weight
of language that tires you, an old world
rolling on the tongue,
replete with grandmothers
and flour-dusted aprons? So, sleep.
The fences along this road fasten
the corners of the fields
and all turns these days seem right.

BLUE BOWL

Warned not to touch,
she touched anyway the first moment
the house lay quiet, the pendulum
regular in its clock case
and no one home—blue leaves
and stems in single brush strokes,
a clear glaze to reflect her face.
What she must have imagined
she held in both hands:
the emperor swaddled in silk,
the Pamirs, snow whiter than bone,
a steady horse easy in its bridle,
a footman, a nurse—who knows
for such porcelain two centuries
had not chipped until she
forgot what she held—
being held so by the gift of her
own mind—and dropped
the bowl.
            She has lived
always in this house
and will remember in her travels
the blossomings and the dying
fires and winter blown
over steps she will climb to find
her way back some evening.
Then she will look down
onto the street in memory, her window
iced, the streetlamp
a blur, the neighbor's oak split
by lightning one summer night
of cicadas and rain.
She will think of porcelain

turned by an old hand,
the wailing she heard
and words clenched tight
as buds in frozen wind,
for the pieces fit when she held them
and the glue took hours
and from then on in a calligraphy
accidental and hers
the seams in her mother's blue bowl
held their delicate
confessions.

THE TORTILLA LINE

The red door is locked,
but everything I think transforms
into tortillas, all laws round,
all r's trilled, accounts settled finally
in tortillas—property and rights
and the proclamations of corn meal
and low fires. What's left today
but to cook fish, meat, and chicken
wrapped with peppers, to relish
the soup with tortillas, to serve them warm
with butter and avocado and sugar.
There is no health without tortillas,
for chills and barber's itch will find me.
Children will cry with their colic
and my neighbors tremble,
their opium and brandy nothing
without tortillas. But with them,
dyspepsia and flatulence, gout and gall stones
will be cured. The delirious
will rise, tend their canaries, clean
mirrors, shake out blankets
in the morning air, their husbands
returned in time to feed
the horses they ride to town
to marvel at its trains,
its plumbers and painters, its experts
who track the lives of birds,
girdle trees, save brooms
and fill cracks with plaster,
who cure sore feet and heaves,
weigh hay by an arm's length
and tax every shingle on my roof.
They wait in line like me

for tortillas wrapped
in terrible news, a single warm
tortilla taken out on the way home
and chewed before the church's
solitary paint-chipped martyr, the hatchet
in his head, a dagger in his breast,
a mirror above him so we might see
ourselves in the eyes of the sainted,
might ponder the fate of the blessed apostles,
how they were hung or boiled
or stoned or flayed or beheaded,
so we might know how difficult it is
to sing with the mouth full.

FITTING

Outside the store my friends
brought me to, marigolds light the walls,
and when we step inside—*bueno*—
the smell of leather, and open hands
settle about my shoulders.
Is there something, I ask, in the color
of smoke rising from the market,
its roasting fires and herbs,
dried lilac and horsetail, a cure
for indigestion or nerves or relatives
discovered by marriage? Something
in the texture of bread stacked
beside the woman who sorts peanuts
and bound, bulbous onions
and red tomatoes and cocoa pods
I mistook for chilies, the bowl
of insects I had no word for?
This morning in the stalls
before weavings, before the shoes cut
from tires, sugar skulls, faces
baked in flour, before the breathtaking
wash of bougainvillea
and cockscomb and cochineal,
I found the length of my reach, stooping
beneath the market's blue sheets
tied against the sun. I sat
and drank coffee as the day dressed
the stone steps around me in hats
and children who stared and raw
cotton bags and baskets of lemons,
and chickens tied at the legs—
meat for today and soup
for tomorrow. All weaving and tobacco,

the air circled, stitched with chatter.
Is there something as light as air
on market day and sound
as the dirt road beneath
our long walk home? Something
kneaded and worked and worn,
something as fitting as today?
I am this wide and this tall.
Of course, they say, and when I raise my arms,
the tailors of Oaxaca
line their mouths with pins.

CORCOVADO

Morenco Biological Preserve,
Osa Peninsula, Costa Rica

When I gave her my name,
howler monkeys started,
their voices bodiless
in green. The moon
assembled insects.
When she called,
I removed my shoes
for the polished wood floor,
for my corner table,
for the woman who set
on cloth before me
cold water and clams
gathered from the Rio Sierpe.
Her apron rustled like wind
beneath the roof,
and when she pointed
along a rafter, moon
after moon rose from a black sea.
No. These were scales,
fine scales when I stood
and held my breath, my eyes inches
from the boa that slept
coiled this evening
above my table, a "she,"
the woman said,
that comes and goes.
I was lucky. When I left
everything behind
and took her offered chair,
and ate and walked each morning
into the forest and swam

in fresh water running beneath
white-faced monkeys
two miles inland and returned
each evening to eat
what I was given, the boa
rested above me.
But the morning I left,
map in hand, the boat waiting
in Drake Bay to take me back
through the mouth of the Rio Sierpe,
its mango roots and vultures,
back through banana plantations
and clear cuts and fires,
I could not find her in the rafters
or palms. She had gone
as the river goes,
winding, I imagine, down
the legs of my chair
and back to the forest to drop and coil
and feed.

WHISPERING IN PENNY'S EAR

For she has slept beside me
  above bags of potatoes and onions
beside old ladies three bunks down
  on the overnight from Brindisi,
and packed suitcases and walked
  the narrow streets lost
in a new language each day
  and washed our socks and hung them
in the window open on a square,
  its tables and coffee and pigeons,
and eaten hard bread or none
  at all and refolded maps and climbed
and descended stairs, walls,
  ruins, streets, and hills, a hand up,
a hand down, each place
  we found amending our idea
of place, blinking and yawning
  each morning between cobblestones
and the ancient blue sky.

For we are telling an old story
  of ourselves that isn't finished,
and for this she waits, sitting
  a moment in Termini station until
I return with tickets
  and schedules and suitcases, my eyes
lifted up to cities rolling by
  on screens. This was my idea, I confess,
and now, dropping my eyes,
  I see her across the station staring
straight ahead, someone
  next to her, leaning on his elbow
to whisper in her ear,

a brilliantined, square-jawed, eyebrow-
arched quoter of Catullus,
    no doubt, in good socks and shiny shoes,
his name ending
    in a vowel, his free hand tracing
roses in the smoky air.

And from the cold north
    I bring for him the history of Rome,
Visigoth and Vandal, the hoards
    come to talk about their taxes, tired
of mud and too few lire,
    having walked for weeks to get here.
And for her I sack the chair
    beside her friend—a senator, I hope—
and lay my bags at his feet
    and fill the air with garlic and onion
and manure and plowed fields,
    the north wind and its intimations
of winter, and shake
    my newspaper open to the want ads
and explain that he will be
    one more chapter in our story, an invitation
he declines and rises, leaving
    an empty chair between her and me and
three days in Rome for us to fill.